*FOOTBALL ON
WASTE GROUND*

FOOTBALL ON WASTE GROUND
Richard Kemp

Published July 2006 by

Smiths Knoll
Goldings, Goldings Lane,
Leiston, Suffolk IP16 4EB

Copyright © Richard Kemp
All rights reserved

ISBN 0-9553314-0-4

After 1 January 2007
ISBN 978-0-9553314-0-4

Typeset at Coachman's Cottage
Printed by Leiston Press, Leiston, Suffolk

Acknowledgements
Thanks are due to the editors of the following publications in which some of these poems first appeared: *Borderlines, The Interpreter's House, The Shop, Smiths Knoll* and *Tears in the Fence*.

Contents

7	Save Us a Place
8	Fireworks
9	Hotelier
10	Off Duty Nurse
11	A Short History of Flight
12	Café on Clacton Pier
13	The Uses of Collecting
14	Sparks
15	Today at a Fountain
16	Fight
17	Why Not Visit
18	Comprehensive Education
19	Real
20	In the Thames
21	What John Hicky Said to Me
22	Rain
23	Yellow Jackets
24	Flour
25	Where is the Man
26	Where is the Woman Who Worked in the Odeon?
27	Football on Waste Ground

Save Us a Place

Lee Gunnery always used to say to me.
'Save us'– for the bus on Wednesday afternoons
when our class went to football.
Killed by something none of us could spell,
he was the jump in the register between Ellison and Higgs.
But still now, he won't have to go on laughing at his own jokes,
become a taller distorted grin.
He won't sneer, look away, searched by a lied-to wife,
struggle to calm a furious secretary.
He won't get a call to say his mother's dead;
be too drunk to sprinkle dirt,
staring at the hole in the ground.
He's still standing by the open goal mouth,
waiting for the corner to come in.

Fireworks

Her perfume was charcoal.
There were no instructions.
I was too young and don't know how I got her.
The first time I took her out nothing happened.
She lived over Mile End Park.
Was it love? I could see her with my eyes closed.
She scared me, kept calling me 'little dog' in bed.
I only wish I could've avoided the pause,
not knowing it was over.

Hotelier

When I was a kid I'd get told off and sent to the conservatory.
I'd smell the cold and look at the tins of carrots, soup, beans
on the old sideboard; and though this was punishment
it was where I first became me,
separate from them in the front room watching television.

You never knew me, though we exchanged smiles
through my little office window on the stairs.
And when you're gone, arguing, making love,
I'm still here – though it's not a shame, it's what I've chosen –
walking the corridors, tracing the flowered wallpaper,
hearing the fan from the factory next door brushing round at night,
sitting back in the chair
watching the skin of my hands yellow under the bulb,
nearly hurting myself on the radiator.

Off Duty Nurse

Her breath turns to steam in the bus shelter;
too tired to smoke, bit-down nails hold an unlit cigarette.
Her blotchy flesh is raw, squashed into cheap plastic shoes.
The red seats weren't made for people to sit properly;
and every little while – through drowsiness – the woman slips;
which would be laughed at by the school kids,
if it weren't for her eyes,
the authority contact with death gives her.

A Short History of Flight

In my room my concern
was how to apply paint to a pilot's hands
without it touching his jacket; to glue in the propeller
on a Dornier, a Hurricane, a Moth,
so it would still turn, this concentration
eased the thought of the beatings,

and not so much that,
but that mum watched.
Lightning, Hellcat, Fury
instructions drew me inches from the magnifier
so I could know these machines,
these escapers

taking off, shooting
over Germany, over France,
wheeling back, on the ends of my arms,
held in, puffed out, like breath;
though my uncle's hands would sweep through,
strafing my hours.

No matter, more kits,
more Saturdays,
more saucers of water,
decals slid off with tweezers,
the country, the type,
Albatross, Spitfire, Hawk.

Café on Clacton Pier

The tables closest to the view
are reserved for people who never come.
The unease I get sitting here is calmed by the miles of sky
seen through twenty foot tall windows.

Most things have changed from that other life,
looking at where the cornicing would've been,
now lit-up with burger signs, though I'm sure the women,
who serve tea like it was their blood, have stayed:
people round here expect that, they must remain.

I dream it all fallen into the sea: the troubled kids,
the women behind the counter, sponging sinking tables
with detergent, their aprons swirling in the waves,
handing me my change (as I drown)
with a perfected lack of generosity.

The Uses of Collecting

On the corner of my old road, Arnburg's
(now a sex shop) gave Green Shield stamps:
my gran let me keep half for sweets.

Later, on Clacton pier we bought coloured wrist bands,
two quid for the day. Sunday might be blue, Monday green,
the day of that colour would come back round
and you could go on everything for free.

Best of all though, Panini Football Stickers,
English and Scottish heads and shoulders, swapped on street corners,
Plymouth Argyle, Bolton, Crewe, shuffled through and argued over,
Man U, Liverpool, in the sit-down part of Tooks the bakers;
and in this devotion
the long days, the trudging to school and our emptiness
after Opportunity Knocks were forgotten.
(We never stuck them in their books)

Sparks

Bill Hailey sings.
The ride smells of oil.
A lad hangs off the back, swinging from car to car,
purposefully ignoring girls looking at him;
taking the steering wheel that a kid can't manage and yanking it.
The dodgem guy is like a dancer,
a beyond-confident force of nature,
present but removed, like the sparks from the grid above.

The same as when I was young.
I wanted to be that bloke; leaning across me to turn the car,
maybe annoyed at having to.
Now I stand in the cold and wait for the train,
see the flash of rails.

    *

I'm friendly with a man who leans on the wall
at the bottom of his flats to talk to anyone who passes,
but mainly to watch the road;
rolls the little wheel of his lighter,
winks at me, shakes it, tries again,
the sparks making the flame, lighting his cigarette,
which I look at. 'It's okay mate,
my lungs have gone already.
I used to work on the fair – my life, *the girls.*'

Today at a Fountain

Two boys play, just stopping from school,
on Lambeth Road, standing up on the metal grill,
jumping then getting soaked. They try to drench each other:
they scoop with cupped hands and throw.
And we all look from the bus like red-framed fish,
we see but we can't connect.
Our retinas are severed from the grey squishy mass.
Their flinging the water back and hiding
are just shop-fronts to us, the walls of the dogs' home
or the station signs we look for.

Far away an ice cream van plays Greensleeves
and no kid will know now it was written by a king.
A plane can be heard, then the rumble of a train, a song from a car;
but somehow today, this day now, when a man asks a girl out
there's a dullness in the sound of his words.
A baby's angry cry is blunt.
Two men fight; but the women at the bus stop aren't bothered,
they complain like yesterday, but now as a duty.
And a boy in the flats is in love with a girl,
they pull each other's clothes, bite each other's faces in small ways,
but all the same cough and come emptily.
Later, in jumpers, they look out at the motorway's bright line,
that now only causes squinting.
On that balcony part of them dissolves.

Fight

The worst fight I ever had was with this sort-of mate,
Paul Bone. I'd chained my bike up next to the pier,
(one of those cheap combination locks
with plastic over the links)
but when I came out it'd gone.

I walked round that dusty town,
sweat itching my neck, missed dinner, went back.
It'd reappeared, carefully placed further along the railings.
And there by the arcade, Bone – I went for him.
He was surprised but kept smiling like a looney tunes.
I was up against a big lad.

He was up against my dad who'd left my mum and now had two kids with another woman, my mum who was in London, my gran (who took over from my mum) who'd had a stroke and couldn't talk properly and had to sleep in the front room, and my uncle who dragged me out to the shed at night to beat me so the neighbours wouldn't hear.

Why Not Visit

Kelvedon Hatch secret nuclear bunker?
Just 20 miles from London, educational and fun for all ages.
Concealed 75 feet under the Essex countryside.
Britain's retaliation would have been authorised from here.
Experience the vast governmental state-rooms.
See the colossal blast doors, to protect the base
and to facilitate its defense if civilians had tried to gain access.
Test your skill at tracking 'a live one'.
See for yourself where the fall-out patterns would have been plotted.
Set in beautiful woodland, with toddler-friendly picnic area.
Visit our gift shop?

Comprehensive Education

At school they walked us along the front at lunchtimes.
One day our headmaster spotted a dead porpoise on the beach.
'Pick it up! Get on with it!' he yelled
at the four of us he sent down there.
So we grappled its slippery skin,
a smooth, hard, awkward bastard,
down Wash Lane to Fuck-face's prize rose bed,
salt water dripping on our shoes.
'Now boys, see those shovels, as a favour to me
chop and dig our friend in, right there by that tree.
I'm at Chelsea next year.'

We looked at each other
but no-one said a word.
So we hacked it, learning.

Real

One day a man walked home from work.
And before he arrived his spirit came in, kissed his wife
while she was looking at the wall above her desk;
this electrical sense in her hair
had the time to look, to touch, to notice
a speck of eye make-up on her cheek
like a black star in a white sky,
before this nothing was swept through
by the real man, making it keener to her,
the fast way he spoke: 'I'm dirty, let me wash.'

Looking up ahead, wondering if his eyesight's getting worse,
he tries to remember his wife's instructions,
what to buy from the shop. He wants to get home for the football.
He doesn't want to have to think, only this traffic
makes him feel he's left at the side of the road
on a verge, just his corpse in the car,
he smiles – it would do well at his job –
but his spirit teeters on a broken wall
high on a hill over Sheffield –
it smells peat, and there are stars –
with no clue how to feel,
slowly, with its arms out, vanishing.

In the Thames

I hear they drag a body up once a week.
People killed, but more usually driven in
by life, as a hammer bangs nails into wood.
I saw a man once,
down by Cleopatra's Needle,
already up to his knees.
Far, far better at Wapping Steps
if you want to go in without an audience.

What John Hicky Said to Me

in St. Joseph's Hospice: 'Well
I wouldn't tell anyone what to do,
as you know, but I'll tell you what *I* do.
I wait.

I eat that...what they give you through there,
I say nothing. I don't worry about Misery Bollocks
in the next bed – *I need a piss! I need a piss!* –
the bane of the nurses. I wait.

It goes like the Marie Celeste in here of a night,
only the girls going up and down.
I'm wide awake, and then I pray.
I ask the Top Man for help. I speak with him.'

Rain

High above night-time shops
lightning flickers, broken television set sky.

Doorways smell our smoke, hear our laughter.
Girls endure our glances.
We are adolescents and will not change,
though laughs transform to coughs, become empty
watery blinks, shaking heads, reminiscences.

It rains in the street. Four decades later
we rub our brows, go on about past beer prices;
the tiredness lifted, so we swear, by the foaming tap,
a pint fresh off the bar: 'Bloody lovely that,
liquid sunshine.'

Yellow Jackets

I see them from the train
through the grimy window, heaving a rail
(I can hardly get my bike up the stairs),
a bank of oaks behind them, coats flapping on a fence.
The light's going; the train stands.
Some men joke around, dusty, unchanged through smoke
from thirty years back and I'm still looking:
they're lowering a flood-lit rail on chains from the sky,
shouting, waving up, catching the horizontal bar,
levelling it to the track-bed, setting it across sleepers
on the crushed granite ballast.
A metal drum burning rotten wood, and the charcoal smell
seeping into the carriage, like old men's yard fires
on my walks back from football.

Ten men, five each side, lift another rail to knee height
before the crane connects, takes the weight.
There's nothing romantic about bastard hard work.
Probably to me they're missing dads…all my mum said:
'He was with the council', that stupid me took to mean
toil in some yard or on a building site seen in passing.

Flour

Until then, except for dusting her wedding photograph
of granddad (who she once knocked out),
I'd never seen her in the front room.
She was in the kitchen; pastry was being made.

Then, on that Tuesday morning no more worry
about us lot back late from the shops,
the hoovering, or my uncle, her son, who drank too much.
Lying in the front room finally, white.

I thought the men who took her were from the bakery
because they had a van.
Beat back the flour men,
why didn't she?

Where is the Man

who slept on the bus back from church on Sundays?
Who spent mornings finding dog-ends to unravel
and pack with hard thumbs into a battered Golden Virginia tin,
the green emblem almost worn off the lid.
Sipping tea from a handleless china cup, the rings unwashed
from each drinking, looking out the window saying 'I'm waiting
for the last few leaves of that bastard bush to fall off
so I can see the road'. Something animal about the old tv guides,
the tv, the chair and the coffee table so close together,
like a nest; watching teletext for dog results
as though monitoring the vital signs of a loved one.

After eating the home help's dinner, staring at the suitcase on the
                                                                                            wardrobe,
granddad made roll-ups like constructing bombs:
a left to right with the tip of the tongue,
a pinch for the excess at the end;
then the smoke unfolded in the milk-light afternoon
gradually, like ink in water, to fill the room,
the nets as yellow as the gold curtains of a shrine
and the ceiling as veined with cracks as a chapel.

Where is the Woman Who Worked in the Odeon?

No more clunk, the big metal ticket machine,
what of it? Crushed down to make another machine.
The rough blue and pink tickets (like recycled paper
before it existed)? Where are the cartons of Kiora?
The Revels, the Butterkist? Do your sovereign rings and crucifix
tarnish somewhere in a shed like the shipwrecked doubloons
in The Crimson Pirate. Your maroon nylon skirt and jacket,
mothballed in a loft or prized by a granddaughter
like a Marilyn gown in a museum?

Your jet black Bela Lagosi hair,
the crushed magnesium black of film sound stock,
the strands of which you'd keep from your glowing white
acrylic blouse, as arctic as your glare.
To be sure (you were Northern Irish) change didn't wait around long
in your hand, it dropped, caught or not;
a crude blue tattoo of a starling between the index and the thumb:
a distant misunderstanding about love?

And what of your bones, let's not leave them out, small and fragile
like the illusion of hope the projectionist (Terry) gave us
in our rows, separated but joined by that flickering beam.
Holes where your eyes were? That looked at sets of double doors
reflecting you back, looking; where people waited outside in the cold
under shiny lights on the steps, and you drew the life from Bensons
in your break. What were you heavy with? Drink got your husband?
No one in the world? The answers are gone with you.
God bless you, gate keeper of that hall painted with stars.

Football on Waste Ground

From a train you see a ball kicked
high, high up, and skinny boys;
there must've been a thud but to you it's silent
and before it falls,
of the three of them, the blond one will be the first to go:
shattered, his blood sprayed across the inside of a car.
The second, ten years after, is held on William Ellis Ward,
has to attend three groups a week,
has put tin foil on the walls round the head of his bed
to stop the government's signals getting him.
And the last one's an impostor:
a father, who goes to work, who comes home, isn't made of wax,
laughs with his mates in the pool hall above the shops,
pretends to his wife
and to everyone,
but his living took place before that ball fell and bounced:
when he could run, feel the cold cutting through to his bones,
and those few dirt square metres were the world.

Richard Kemp was born in Luton in 1970 and grew up in Clacton. He studied Psychology and Art in London, at Birkbeck College and Central St. Martin's School of Art, followed by an MA at Sussex University, whilst working as a care assistant and youth worker. He currently works as a drugs counsellor in East London.

This is the first in a series of pamphlets to be generated by the innovative **Smiths Knoll Mentoring Scheme**, funded by Arts Council England East. The scheme is designed to accelerate the development of a promising poet, chosen by the editors for the quality of their submissions to the magazine. It runs in each case for a full year and offers detailed feedback on work in progress via email and face to face meetings.